T0105705

FOURTH DIMENSION

FREE SPIRITED SPOKEN WORD IN WRITTEN FORM

MARCUS "THAREAL KIDD" CURETON

IUNIVERSE, INC.
BLOOMINGTON

Fourth Dimension
Free Spirited Spoken Word in Written Form

iUniverse books may be ordered through booksellers or by contacting:

iUniverse
1663 Liberty Drive
Bloomington, IN 47403
www.iuniverse.com
1-800-Authors (1-800-288-4677)

Because of the dynamic nature of the Internet, any Web addresses or links contained in this book may have changed since publication and may no longer be valid.

ISBN: 978-1-4502-7981-9 (sc)
ISBN: 978-1-4502-7982-6 (ebk)

Printed in the United States of America

iUniverse rev. date: 10/13/2009

N.I.G.G.A.

This commonly used word [Nigga] by rappers, hip-hopsters, young African Americans and Urbanized society is not to be confused with the word Nigger.

The word Nigger -which in the early dictionaries- means an ignorant person. At least we know who made that definition, huh? Well, shall I say that this word was given to us by white America to downgrade us in the worst way possible back in slavery days! They were trying to brain wash us into believing that we were less than the crud at the bottom of their foot wear.

The word 'Nigger' was derived from a place and a river titled Niger which is located in the continent of Africa. The Niger River flows 2,600 miles from Guinea through Mali, Niger, and Nigeria into the Golf of Guinea. This is also a place where traders would travel with slaves as they used Africans as a product to move them all over the globe, thus giving us the name that has taunted the true power behind our existence then and today.

We as a people of the African decent take offense to this word because of what it stands for; much more than any dictionary could try to describe. This word creates tears and misogyny in our hearts. Being as we are, a strong race and people, a newer generation of us has taken that word and bent it. Twisting its natural meaning and formed this word N.I.G.G.A. It could mean just what the late rapper Tu-Pac said, "*Never ignorant and getting goals accomplished ...*" or it could be embraced as the analytical term of my fellow brothers of the struggle -like most young black men explain it to be. We may never know; but it still will create some type of argument, fierce emotions, disappointment and disagreement within the African American culture and many others.

Now, I don't want you to embrace this word if you have not done it already, but I just ask that you don't take offense to it as you come across it in this book or any other of my works. I merely use it to describe the particular emotions of anger and heart felt demeanor in this book. We all have to express ourselves some way; sometimes it's with words that need not be used. Thank you and May God be with us all!

CONTENTS

Section Four
My epiphany of direction

Section five
A true eye opener / I see clearly now

Section Six
Final call / Keeping strong

Acknowledgements

INTRODUCTION

What's My Art

It's that system of rhythm, artistic criticism and deep down reprimand of a life long agenda;

I saw no justice for all, first I stood up then had to fall, and then everyone could see it in my walk;

Long strides in my days as I ran in that maze, while trapped in my cage, and then finally woke up out of my daze;

Then I heard it as it was calling and stood up after falling, standing firm on my feet because I had a mission to complete;

I didn't give in to defeat, because I knew that history would repeat;

I released the safety and reloaded, just aimed at my goal …

Pulled the trigger and let go … [Blaaaaaaaaw!]

SECTION ONE

EYE OPENER

THE COURAGE TO ACHIEVE A DREAM

What a light beyond the end of my path which seems so bright and gloomy,

And it seems like a light at the end of a tunnel in a dramatic movie;

I've lived this dream day in and night out which seems to slowly linger,

For a dying dream is only a dream once ones mind weakens the finger;

But I believe and have the faith right now to overcome any adversity,

And I know that I must continue this path to achieve my dreams deepest capacity;

For a goal is only a planed out dream that has many orderly steps,

And to accomplish that goal the most important step is the dedication that must be kept;

Then persistence and patients are two more steps that falls along that path,

And the ambition to pursue the very next level is something that I must have;

I almost forgot this one more step which is the courage to follow through,

I know there's no such thing as a false dream because every dream can come true;

But they only can happen if I believe and know that it can be achieved,

For a dream is more when I adore the essence within that dream!

WALK INSTEAD OF TALK

The miracle of following your own passionate dreams
Is to reap the rewards of your works
To live up to your own positive standards
Is to reveal a hidden agenda within self …
So know what you are truly capable of achieving …
Anything your heart desires and you're seemingly over reactive dreaming

Following through is to know what you really can do
In a world where many have dreams
But when you verbally expose your mind they laugh at you …
So you know what you must do!

Put actions to your thoughts and walk instead of talk
That road which many dream of
But don't have the courage to stand up and walk tough

Seeing is the results of believing in self when you knew that you would make
it …
Every time you slip and fall you stand up and beat your feet across the
pavement
While never letting anyone capture your dreams in a stage of enslavement
Then you will come to achievement and look back then say …
"I finally made it … Damn it feels so good!"

So knowing that you can stand firm and strong on your own dreams
Is better than never putting an action to a goal you once made and briefly
attempted to see …

The honor lives within you to never let go …
Of a dream you have passion for
And a reality you want to know.

ETHICAL AFRO- AMERICAN

Strong in might and the darkest of the night
Persistent, brilliant and determined in the fight ...
Willing to conquer with vigilance, so vigor
Never down-grading ones self to that so called word 'Nigger' ...
Driven, confident and conscious of self
Prestigiously accepting the title 'Preserver' by always giving help ...
'Uplifting' and embracing another sista' or brotha'
Recognizing true pigment in the reflection of another ...
Efficiently combined and in sync with each other
Parental guidance to the youth like a father or mother ...
Helping each other because we're strong together
Progression of a race that will always be clever ...
Developing our youth to be generational heroes
Knowing that we are a pure outstanding people ...

RAINY THOUGHTS ON A RAINY DAY

Rain …
I see it coming
It's beating upon my head …
The streams down my face let me know the race has just begun
Entering the arms of mine
As a new face paints a picture in time
Embracing love as I continue to move forward
With no thoughts of ever looking behind …

My rearview is so clear too
I can't bend, brake or fold …
I got big goals and big dreams so I must stay on the go …
Who was the liar that said history repeats itself …
They surly weren't talking about me because I got big help …

A new mind, a new me, yeah I transformed
From the epitome of crime, so watch me now perform …

Like Shakespeare the world is my stage, I'm about to turn it out
Kick down some doors in this race, blow out the flames now …
No room for eras, I can't stumble while on this march
Pick up the youth, spit some truth and just go hard …

Just let them know where I come from and what I've been through
"This aint no game, this aint a joke, and I'm here to help you!"

Got every intention of doing right but I still think wrong
"No one wants to hear this 'poetry stuff', it aint going to last long!"

Big doubts and new routes, thinking about doing the same stuff
"Flip some bags, to a piece, and then I can ride tough …!"
But I know the things that I've been thinking is just lunacy
If I go back to hustling the odds are against me …
So I'll continue to walk down this rainy road
And know that just ahead of me are lots of rainbows …
With new suns and new skies
Yeah, there are some brighter days …
I'll keep my head up through this walk and just continue to pray …

SOUL SEARCHING

Looking for something that's deep down within,
Trying to get rid of a bundle of sins;
Turning my life to a whole new path,
It takes a lot of time, if only I could do the math;
I feel pain in my heart from past wrong doings,
At once I felt my life was really ruined;
Now, I look up and stand straight tall,
Knowing my life will go on and don't fall;
Reading more books and enhancing my brain,
I know my life will never be the same;
Looking for something that only I can bring out,
It's not an easy task walking this life route;
I pray that the Lord gives me strength to move on,
Life is to short and I can't prolong;
I'm trying to figure out just what my task in life is …
Maybe it's to love and also love to live …

Life is full of difficult tasks
And many strange directions!

CONVOCATION

The blood of Africa bled on these states as they forced us to pave their way,
And we fought and fought to stand face to face with equivalence upon each race
Now we're as close as ever but we are constantly tearing each other down
While degrading ourselves through gangs of negativity, violence and putting our own people in the grounds
"Now, I don't want you to think that I'm a hypocrite but I've finally come to realize
"That my past criminal history and the pain that I've caused were lack of self-knowledge and being uncivilized …
"So I apologize!"
Let us take a deep breath and open our hearts and strive for togetherness to arise …
The time is now to come together …
So brothas' and sistas' …
"Let's open our souls, minds and eyes!"

SUCH SIGHTFUL BLINDNESS

Seeing imperfection in societies mirror of injustice as my eyes constantly stare at my own reflection

Trapped in the Fourth-Dimension as this moment shows resistance with no assistance I try to prevail and overcome

After years of freedom craving my feet finally touched the pavement no more enslavement but I still got to eat

So now this is where I stand when everyone said "It's time to be a man!" but the streets are the only way that I know how to eat ...

And there death still waits for me ...

"BUT UNTIL THEN MY EYES ARE STILL WIDE THE HELL SHUT!"

A TALK WITH THEE INEVITABLE

All these years that I have feared you, you were inevitable in every sense
All those times that I've denied you, you lingered around when I'd repented
And every time when I could sense you, cold chills ran across my flesh
So now that you are creeping near me, I surly can't rest …
Every time I close my eyes I get the feel of what you're about
I hold my breath and act 'as if' of you, then I quickly let it all out
Just the sight of you upon others faces had me surly afraid to trade places …
Now all my fear erases …
I know that you're there and I don't care
And I know your actions because I've always been aware
I fear you no more and ask what you will do …
But yet and still you don't make a move
So I'll just continue to do what I need to do
And as you try to creep when you think that I'm asleep …
Of course I'll notice you …
Hell, I might even embrace you …
"Death …!"

WARS WITHIN
OUR PEOPLE

Chant* Another fatherless child, no love in this house, relations times two
and I don't know what to do, Come help me, come help me, come
help me pave truth!!! [Save the youth!]

I've tried to hide and deny who you said that I was,
But the streets didn't birth me they just raised me into a thug;
Gang-banging, selling cane and representing with my click,
And I've seen to many die in this gangsterfied' flick;
"Who you be?" and "What you is?" blue and black or black and red,
Pistol smoking, six or five and tears cried for the dead;
When you represent by carrying the name you gang-bang to maintain,
Then you do what you do like 'Do or Die' by upping' thangs …
I've seen some on the hustle on the grind for new things,
Getting drunk, smoking weed and doing more drugs like Ecstasy;
Pistol totting, big guns, 'On that lane!', 'Here comes the Feds!' …
Yo' block, ma' block, our hood, the projects;
From the slums of the gutters, the crack houses and dope fiends,
Yo' sista', his motha' and ma' aunty feeding me green;
Now they're the neighborhood zombies, walking dead and motionless,
Got me pushing new whips with big rims and getting rich …

[Chant]*Another fatherless child, no love in this house, relations times two
and I don't know what to do, Come help me, come help me, come
help me pave truth!!! [Save the youth!]

I thought I'd finally found me …
When I was once a lost child caught in these gangs in these streets
Up'd the piece, cocked the heat, [Blaaaaw], leaving blood in these streets …
Confusion, a nuisance, I was lost to my lunacy …
A young street punk the old timers use to call me.
"And they were right!"

No direction, I was missing a father figure in my life
Then I found myself repeating the same cycle as my [sperm donor] father
On the other side of the pipe feeding rocky substances to my sistas' and brothas'
Got two children by two different baby mothers
Divided homes, can't get along, and just moving along to another …

[Chant]* Another fatherless child, no love in this house, relations times two
and I don't know what to do, Come help me, come help me, come
help me pave truth!!! [Save the youth!]

History aint teach us this, where have we went wrong?
Living in our own ignorance and passing it down to our young
Minority and majority, we got ourselves all discombobulated
Our communities now lack unity and who's to blame for this miscommuni-
cation … "Besides self?"
Our loses are their gains double the times …
Killing each other as we constantly commit these crimes …
And not handing down our history to those fruitful minds …
The battle is on day in and night out but what we've been doing has set us apart
We better try harder to pick ourselves up because we're not winning …
"They are!!!"

[Chant]* Another fatherless child, no love in this house, relations times two
and I don't know what to do, come help me, come help me, come
help me pave truth!!! [Save the youth!]

BIG TIMA'

Put a lil' pimp in yo' step
Some limp in yo' step
From gangsta' to soulja, nigga' you know where you at
So what's yo' status quota, I heard you rolling in doe and a nigga' can't sale a
bag because you got the block sold
Got niggaz' pockets on hold, you hood rich I was told
From gutter to glamma, you banging hammers I'm told
Dropping niggaz like fly's because you determined to rise
You don't let a soul get in yo' way and you know I aint surprised
And when the law had a tail you just covered yo' trail
Doing everything in yo' power to duck that jail cell
But once that gavel struck the bench you saw what you had at risk
Leaving everything behind for a thirty year stint …

IMAGES

Not knowing what the future holds when there is so much on your shoulders
at the present time
Visionary images of insane thoughts of not seeing tomorrow when your body
is lying in chalk

What to do in this situation is what you ask yourself
Thinking won't do much because your mind is stuck

Stuck, stuck

Stuck in a faze that brings your actions to a blaze
That has your mind in a maze
Which forms your visual essence as of a daze

Daydreaming over and over
Your mind is very sober on thoughts that brings reality to a halt
Then everything around you is misunderstood from the past tense

What you've done to bring yourself
To this friction in the present
But I really think of it as a blessing

You could be gone to another state of immortality
Or is it death

Death is the easy way out
But who knows what the Lord has planned
Continually telling yourself that you are in command of your life

If you are in command then why are you here?
Stuck in a place of nasty rituals in waste

And corruption in the eyes of those you face
And receiving a bit of your own medicine

Life, life, life
This is life
"So wake up …"

SECTION TWO
A PIECE OF MY HEART

MY ADDICTION

Damn I want it, damn I need it …
To feel it, to touch it, to breathe it …
It's like a drug to me; your love is all I need, which fulfills me completely …

To feel the presence of love in its purest form turns my cold low days into high days, making them warm …

It's my addiction …

Using the world as my pond as I go fishing,
Seeking and searching like a crack addicts fixing …

Because you know I need it, and you know I crave it
So when you open up to me you know I have to enslave it …
Capturing its real true beauty and essence
Because I only crave you pure hearts presence

Not just any love will do, your heart has the only love that feels true
Pulling me up when I feel so blue, because of the craziest things that I will do …
For your love …

Without it shivers takes its toll and I begin to lose control
Just because your love molds me, so baby save me …

This addiction has enslaved me and the only cure is for you to love me …
So baby, open up to me …

I'm dying inside without you baby, so are you going to be my sweet lady and rescue me …

This addiction is eating me alive so why does your love tries to hide away from me …

Knowing that I want it, knowing that I need it
So just open your heart so I can embrace it …

Only to mend the wounds of my scarred heart and cure this addiction …
Because I need that fixing …

TEACH ME

Teach me to love you the way you need to be loved
Show me how to touch you in ways that I can never imagine
Give me the power to fulfill your every desire by satisfying your physical and mental wires ...

"Teach me baby!"

Communicate with me by verbally telling me how to be the man you want of me ...
Show me how to fulfill your fantasies baby ...
Give me access to the doors in your mind so that I can unlock them with my keys of intentions to love you the way you deserve to be loved

Let me show you just how much I love you by pleasing your heart and mind
Let me show you just how much I care for you by being of value to your spirit and soul

See ... without you, this lonely heart of mine is lost in the abyss of the cold
And when I'm near you it seems to regain a sense of control ...
All from the bitter separation of you and my lost soul

Yes ... now I feel whole
Because you have given me hope that you will teach me to touch beyond your soul ...

And when you quiz me with your physical and mental intimate tests I'll be able to take control
Just because you taught me how to be what you need in life ...

So ... whenever you feel as if I am not completing the task at hand
Don't hold back just tell your man ...!

Show me what your heart is yearning
And I guarantee I'll keep your urging desires burning ...
As long as our hearts will forever more beat
We both should know that all of the above is a two way street

So we both now know what to do ...
You teach me and I'll teach you ...

A FOOL FOR LOVE

Damn love, where have you been?
I've been seeking for you to dwell within ...
These four walls of my heart which shows the meaning of my essence
But that purity of your power shows aggression
Once that entity that I seek shows neglection
But then you want to tell me that you were just testing me ...
"What's up with that?"

You know that my heart and mind is fully erect and set ...
On you to be what you've always been
A love that sticks through thick and thin and will always be there until the
bitter end
Now my heart sees that it was a sin ...
To love you ...

So is foolishness the answer to that, because I'm so crazy to keep taking you
back ... into my heart?

Damn love, I truly loved you from the start and you made life for me so
hard
Now I ask that is it suspect to say that love is at large once again
And do I go back to you once again and suffer from this thing all over
again ...
I doubt that ...!

Damn ... you just caught me right back in your trap and I'm running in
circles in this lab like a rat, now I find myself constantly suffering from that ...
same old thing in the same old places
Pushing myself into the same old repeated races ... for love ...!

Asking myself, "Why do fools fall in love?"
Is it because we all are fools for love?
Or is it because I was a fool for your love?

OBLIVIOUS LOVE

Can a letter lead a person into a brick wall when one heart is seeking the others mate call?

Secretes, your meekness disguised what it was, when carrying is cherished cloaked with love

Ambivalent, confusions gives my heart contusions which makes me believe you finagled my love … all the while you were finessing your way with kisses, passion and hugs

You swindled and twist me like a serpent at deep sea once it squeezes the life from its pray

I'm crushed and all broken like a ship that is sunken once it's struck by a stone off the bay

My chest is still caving from bitterness and slaving because I wanted you to accept me in whole

You tell me you love me but not from what I see when you buried my heart in a hole

Don't tell me you love me then run when I'm falling because you fear to trust in my love

So I guess my strength is your weakness which leaves me insomnious those nights that my body craves sleep

Infuriated delusions has my mind with confusion when emotions is all my heart seeks

From responses to letters I sent but you cleverly rip shreds through my heart … so unique

A love doctor you claim but you caused my heart pain so step back if you can't handle this

Now you're ranting and raging about my heart is caving but can't you see that you're causing me stress

So it's distance, not nearness to a love that is fearless from the impact of your heart of cement

You hoodwinked my soul and left me motionless in the cold so my reactions is to return a great favor
Those nights when we're in an act of coition I'll show great persistence towards fulfilling my intimate mission

Then your heart will have wondered of the warmth it has plundered while savoring its beautiful flavor ...
Then slowly I'll stray and just walk straight away from a spouse that tends to now cater!

KEEPING IT REAL

A day without you drags forever
And turn my clear days to very stormy weather
But the image of you sticks deep within my thoughts
This gives me courage to keep my head up through this walk
I know I'm never alone because your love is there
Sheltering me and showing me that you care
From every letter to every call
To those 'I love you's' tells it all
But words really can't express how I feel
Because for me to show you is to keep it real

STRAIGHT FORWARD

Would I be wrong if I told you my needs?
A long craving for love that's past overdue
And I'm noticing what I crave is deep inside of you …

So, what are you going to do?
Will you conclude my cravings by letting me be with you?
Or will you ignore the blessings within this suggestion, knowing that my cravings are the same as yours
And afraid to give in because you fear real love?

What if I could fulfill your every desire?
By reaching your heart and taking you higher … than life?
We could sail amongst the stars while seeking the moon
And bounce through the galaxy like two flying harpoons

Just take your time and don't make up your mind to soon
I know that your heart has been caged like a cocoon
And now it's ready to explode and show its true beauty
Showing me that deep within you lives more than just a cutie

Your actions speaks louder than any words
Taunting me in my dreams and raveling my nerves

I can tell that you want to oblige
From that pause and the look in your eyes … that speaks for the core of your essence
You have to be my better half which makes you more than a blessing

So I can't let this opportunity past me
I'm seeking and assuming that you will be my sweet lady

So baby … don't leave me hanging …
Because true love only comes once in a life time
So to put the ball in your court I ask one question …
"Will you be mine?"

CONVERSING SOULS
HIM AND HER

Him: Just how bright do you think a star can shine when it is compared to
you …?
No shiver of a glimmer like a ripple in the sky or a pebble that strikes the
      water which no longer dries
      "That star holds no weight!"
      Gases no longer burns as they implode while in space
      Like the jumbled emotions I receive when we greet face to face …
      Your skin is like the softness of a flower blooming near the sea at
      night
      The calmness of the moon that bares no fright
      But alone a star sits in the sky like a kite
      And when I'm close to you your shine is more bright
      So don't be afraid …
      No … I won't bite …
      I just want to get to know you a bit better …
      Then maybe 'You' and 'I' can truly become 'We' …
      "So what do you think?"

Her: What if I accept your offer and we embrace in eternal fate …?
      Will you desert me and leave my side because love didn't reap what it
      anticipated …?
      And what about sex, did you know that I was abstinent?
      Do you think that you can wait until marriage has made reproduction
      relevant …?
      Yes, I feel what you feel when my emotion overflow
      And when your arms are around me my heart overloads and feel like
      it will explode …
      So I accept that my shine is bright but yours could be brighter
      By meaning what you say and together we both can go that much
      higher …
      The Sun brightens the day and the Moon does the same to the night
      If we were to take that step then we both will be those lights …
      Now I told you what I feel without fear and the rest is left up to you
      I accept the responsibilities of being your Sun but what do you think
      about being my moon …?

Him: I will never leave you and will always have your back
   Nor will I deceive you or cause your heart to crack …
   "True love knows its boundaries!"
   So being your Moon is what I'll do by accepting your invitation
   And proving to you that my love is true by honoring your abstinence
   and showing you patients …
   Now 'You' are my Sun and 'I" am your Moon which makes 'We' a
   complete day
   Since we agree and are on the same page there shouldn't be more to
   say …

Her: Besides me taking your hand right now just before we make an eternal
   embrace …
   And let love show us the way …
   As surly as these 'I do's' escape our lips under divine source
   'You' and 'I' will become a force …
   In 'We' …

SHE LAWS

"The accountabilities of actions that I take is enforced through feminine eyes
But if anything hold me accountable for being in love before I die
And how would she do this when she is constantly searching for my flaws
I just bend the rules a little for love but she says I'm breaking the laws
What about all the good that I've done, do she credit me for that
Oh no, she wants to see me rot for bouncing a loveless check
So am I wrong for providing her love and do I have any regrets …
No, out of all the women that I've been with, she the one who I'm glad I met
She showed me what true love was about and how it really felt
Bringing passion to the surface of my mind and she caused my heart to melt
No other woman in my past can amount to what she's done
And if loving a person was a race to the finish she's the one who surly won
So, if being in love with a person like I am with her is against any laws
I'd do a life sentence in her sight because she's the one who my love last saw!"

GET AT YOU

Your jazzy smile and that persona about you make me feel that you got it going on, and I got to approach you and speak these words that I really can't prolong …

Your casual style of dressing is really testing and got me puzzled while thinking that you're very interesting, with your long sleek dress and that cleavage cut blouse which reveals your beaded necklace …

Those heels you're wearing is creating a tearing in my heart, from the way your calves and thighs are raised you're making life for me so hard …

Your soft humble voice brings shivers down my spine, and your smooth textured skin just blows my mind …

So damn girl, what can I say besides I want to get at you, and just tell me if you're down or not because one plus one makes two … not a group, just me and you …

If you're wondering what I see in you I'm going to break it down like this, your sex appeal gives me the chills and the feel that you can be real with it …

So what's the deal …?

I just want to be the man that you can feel … and when others are being fake to you, I want to be the man who's real to you, no lies and games pure uncut truth …

So baby what are you going to do?
Are you going to go to someone fake?
Or will you embrace this truth coming to you?

600X CM

Endless tunnels in the abyss of my soul,
As departure shows existence without permission to be exposed;
Missing the presence of oneness when two is a whole,
Because her love had strayed when her heart turned cold;
My heart was like glass when she smashed it on the floor,
As the cuts in my flesh left my mind to explore …
Abrasions and bruises left my mind with contusions,
Going crazy convincing self that it was an illusion;
Madness, insane, as my soul feels this pain,
In a place where emotions all now feel the same;
I need guidance and direction,
Not a path of perfection,
But a road that mends my wounds and cures this neglection;
Like shooting fire at deceit,
A twelve on one struggle when I defeat …
A tribe of a dozen more emotions …
My nose was open like the ocean,
Mind was floating like I was smoking,
And heart was thumping like a bucket in front of the downtown Local
Motive …
Pushing speeds that exceeds brand new Ferrari's,
Sixty in point three,
Showering her in jewelry,
And giving her what she needed,
When all she needed was just me,
In this world where she could have anything and everything…
But now I see her intentions so clearly …
Under loves microscope of today's reality.

I CAN'T TAINT

I got a jones in my bones for this Nubian princess named Simone
And it just eats me to the core of my soul ... [fa'real]

You aint heard me, so let me take you home ... [Preach!]
She got hair that's pitch black as her locks falls down her back
And a walk that takes up for anything that she lacks ... [Umph, um, um!]

Her caramel skin is so smooth and I don't know what to do every time she
comes around in my presence ... [Alright!]

I say, her voice is so soft when she speaks as she walks a melody sticks within
the core of my essence ... [Talk about it!]

Bamboo beads, Kenta' cloths, koofi hats and dashiki smocks, yeah, she's
deeply in touch with her roots ... [Well!]

I love to see her smile as my emotions tends to run wild, thinking, will our
hearts and minds ever get into cahoots ... [What!]

Will our souls coincide and maybe one day she'll be my bride, is the thoughts
that I think when she arrives ... [Okay!]

See, she's a dime plus more who I really adore and to me sista-girl is the true
meaning of purity ...

Her charisma, integrity, and intelligence when she speaks intrigue this jones
in my bones, but I know we could never be ... [Damn, why not?]

See, I'm the scum of the earth, filthier than dirt, and just as slick as grease can
be ... [So what!]

She's one of a kind, very hard to find and deserves to be with much more
than me;

Yes, I'd love to be in love with her and would care to worship her, but I know
what would happen in time ...

I'd be imprisoned of a crime of turning pure water into bitter wine ...
To taint such beauty as this queen who I would love to me mine!

JUST HOW FAR WOULD YOU GO

Why do you doubt me when I have given you proof
Like verbal explanation that can only be true
Do you think that I would lie to you?
And because of this, am I the one that you despise too?
What do I have to do to prove my loyalty to you?
Do I need to sign this paper with my blood for you?
Just so you can understand pure truth

I would literally walk naked over the peeks of snowed in mountains just to
seek frozen fountains, you see …
If you had told me that your love would be there waiting on me
Just so I could unlock your heart's mystery
This is to show you that my love has no boundaries …
When it comes to the passion that my heart constantly seeks … from you
So tell me what's the answer that lingers is in your passionate mind when I ask
what do you know … about how far would you go …
For me!

SECTION THREE
FLIP THE SCRIPT /
JUST THE HEART OF A GANGSTA'

Ma' Hood

When one chooses to be
Apart of the solution,
The problem becomes
That much curable.

TRU' FEARS

I don't mentally want to go back to the streets,
But if a Nigga' run up I'm going to have to up that piece;
And stand firm on my own two feet,
Might have to blast me a Nigga' and put him six feet deep;
Then I'd be back down trying to work from a sixty-three to a ki,
Puffing Swisher Sweets with goals of driving big ole Bentley's;
Geared from head to toe, dressed to the 'T',
Chain iced to death and my wrist so frosty,
Now I'm back down and feeling more like a 'D';
With my Buck-Fifty Wing Ding hat broke to the right and the bezel iced out,
This is my fear as I get closer to getting out …

The game is calling my name and it's getting louder,
And it's steady causing me pain as I think about that powder …
Pyrex on the stove as I watch that stuff mode;
Then take that hanger and push it all on a chilled plate,
After it rock up, I bag it up, feeling like this is my fate;
As the king steps up to his royal place,
And selling bags that are so big I'm giving them more than a taste …

Then I'd be back down as I set myself to come back to this place …
Prison cells, locked doors and steel weights …
Seeing a corn field, a tower and express-way through a gate …
As these thoughts past through my mind my heart fills with hate;

So when I touch down I aint got no time to waste,
I got to stay focused out there and think straight;
By setting new values, new goals, and keeping faith …
Then legitimately find a way to paper chase.

IF YOU WANNA' STRAP UP

You don't want to see gangsta' …
Mess around and get messed up
I'm that Nigga' from the E-Dub who aint afraid to get buck;
But if you keep pushing my buttons you bound to be the first to luck up …

Lock up, toe-to-toe and blow for blow, I'm going to get mine,
Left nut, upper-cut and head-buts will leave you blind;
Blood gush, your face mush on the ground at the curve,
Lights out, one bout, it's messed up you had the nerves;

Many years in the hood, you know I lived in this pit,
Another crime, another time, I aint about to do anymore bids;
But if it's our life, our fight, either you or me,
Head to toe, no cover up, cast you six feet deep;
Then my adrenaline gets to flowing, I aint got nothing to lose,
Hold court on the streets or go to jail, pick or choose;
So, to avoid these actions stay the hell out of my way,
The joint aint on my agenda so take short breaths and pray!

I'M HUNGRY TOO

I want to shine if I got to grind,
I'm that Nigga' from the streets flipping lit lick a crime …
From in the joint scribbling bar after bar to ease my mind,
Composing myself as I set still in time …

Only to reap the still waters of the streets,
Where as another one of my brother's is dying from heat …
If not that they end up being the cause of the beef,
Where the young has no hesitation to kill the old so they can so call eat …

"These niggaz' dun' lost their minds …!"

That's what the elderly say when they think back in time,
And what they got to understand is that the stakes are higher and evolution
has brought new age crime …
But that still don't justify the things that we're doing to reap penitentiary time …
All to get the crumbs from a paper trail that another player in the game left
behind …

All the while they still tell themselves "I got to eat!"
Well, I will tell them "You do that mess and I will do me!"

While I'm accomplishing my line of goals after touching back down with a
new reality, my game is going to reach its peek …
Hit the bricks with my mental keenness on charge in those streets,
And pitching dime pieces of this 'Lit' so my oppositions can't compete;
Getting rid of jabs of thirty out my back pack, so unique;
Seeing the fiends posted around the corners and knowing they seek me …
See, I know what I got to do …
Say good bye to that old thing and get with this new 'Lit' because I'm hungry too!

[That old way is dead to me. There's no such thing as
"One way or another" when it comes to the dope game.
Only one way exists in my mind today, the right way.
So, I'm shooting my shoot … "I got to eat because I'm
hungry too!"]

OPEN YOUR EYES GANGSTA'

Gangsta', gangsta' can't you see, with your ski mask on and your hands so bloody ...
"Mr. Stick up man, a killer in disguise, why must they die?"

I just murdered a whole family within a blink of an eye;
As I walked cold heartedly with piercing dagger eyes I noticed a crying stutter,
Looking in the corner of a closet, balled in a tight wad is a crying child in the arms of its mother ...
With no hesitation I put a bullet in both of their heads, but her tennis bracelet that was full of diamond begets caught my vision ... now I must complete my mission;

One yank as I broke the clip and walked out in one motion, picked up my bag of cash and kept on pushing;
With no thoughts as I walked about what I just done, then I wiped the handle clean and tossed my gun;
I then pulled away my mask and rolled up my gloves, and tossed them in the trash as I walked away with greed in my blood ...

Shyster and conniving to take what I want kill or be killed, either you do or you don't;
What's left now is to count my cash, as I sat at the table smoking weed then basked;
Suddenly something bothered me across the room on my tube, the picture of my victims on the ten o'clock news;
Then fear overcame me as I turned the news up, and sat down as I began to roll me another blunt up;

"Stop the violence!"

They chanted to receive a positive reaction, and I thought the weed was playing tricks with my mind when I saw Jesse Jackson;

"We must lift each other up and increase the peace!!!"

I said look at this Nigga' as I gritted my teeth;
But just at that moment they flashed another picture of my victims,
A black child, mother and a father that was with them;
Then pain and remorse came barreling down, as I thought about all the black on black crime that exists in my town ...

"I am the main supplier and the soul provider of all this black on black crime!"

As that thought came across my mind I fell to my needs as I heard a voice say "It's about time!"

I pulled out my gun and put it to my head as I pulled the trigger with no hesitation ... "Click" no action as I lacked satisfaction to pursue this situation ...
To rid the world of a disease like me, I deserve far more then the penitentiary;

So I extracted the clip to check my ammunition, fully loaded to proceed on with my mission;

Closed my eyes as a tear rolled down my face, raised the barrel to my head as my hand began to shake;

Said a quick prayer as I began to pull the trigger, and then an angel appeared in front of me and said ... "open your eyes Gangsta'!"

A BIT OF REFLECTION

Let me commune by the new noon and give you a piece of me that needs to
be exposed
A dark child from a cold past of these streets that you may call the ghetto
Reminiscing about times when food was like a delicacy
When I was just a small child running the streets that was full of poverty
Visions of brick phones strapped over shoulders and Apple garage door
openers on hips ...
And those smooth but cool words came off of the drug dealers lips
A buck in my pocket as I shoot off like a rocket to Mrs. Mary's candy house
on the corner ...
You know I had to get those Jolly Joes, Slap Sticks and those Caramels
Shirt filthy, pants sticky, as I wiped my nose with my sleeve ...
Walked through the door as I stepped over trash on the floor and had no food
on the table or in the pantry;
Opened the refrigerator as I observed it being just about empty, then I
grabbed that bread from the back and added sugar with cheese to substitute
for meat ...
That was my meal for the night; I thought it was right eating wish sandwiches ...
"Do you think that this is unique?"

First of the month that government cheese was added to everything, had that
cheese toast with sugar on top and that Kool-Aid that was surpy sweet,
That pork in the can from the church on the corner and that powder milk ...
yes it was also sweet ...
These were like rich days, that first of the month, growing up in poverty ...
Looking back in time as my mind unwinds vivid pictures tends to shine ...
A realization of ones true past seems to reveal who I now am, from what was
to now as I recount a part of what brought me to the present ...
I lived a life that was so misconstrued, but I still think of it as a blessing ...

"Damn!"

I'M NOT GOING BACK

*[I'm not going back, I got to keep pushing forward, and I'm not going back,
through the grace of the Lord...]*

It's a new start for me to do what I got to do, leaving the penitentiary saying
"Forget my crew!"
I know it's hard but I got to face the truth, that dope game and that gang-
banging, yeah I was true
But I got to leave it all behind for the sake of my kids, or else I'll be back in
that pen doing another bid
I said I change my life so I got to do what's right, there's already too many
black kids without a father in their lives
So I'm going to break that chain of cycle and be there for my kids, and these
people will have one less black man doing a bid
As I walk through these streets it is tempting man, to jump back down and
start back carrying that pistol in the land
But I know for every temptation there is a bad result, so I will try to leave the
whole game lying in the chalk
And you should know that it's hard for the Kidd in this white mans world,
trying to provide for my son and my baby girl
But I will do what I have to do and that's a fact, because thoughts of not being
near my kids make me say "I'm not going back!"

*[I'm not going back, I got to keep pushing forward, and I'm not going back,
through the grace of the Lord...]*

See, the good Lord gave me a gift and that's my freedom, as I sat in the court
room in trial I thought I couldn't beat them ...
But he proved me wrong and at the same time he proved me right, because
our heavenly father showed up in a time of need in my life
So I thank him for that blessing like everyday, and I know when times get
hard he'll tell me "It will be okay!"
Every time I look up I see someone dying or going to jail, which makes me
believe that this world is a step before Hell
That's another reason I tell myself "I aint going back to the streets," because
of my old mentality I had to make sure I packed my heat
But that will just be setting me up for the law to get back at me, so I'm going
to try to leave it alone so I can avoid the extra heat

I'm already on parole and these people got me on a leash, which makes it harder for me to get a job and wondering how am I going to eat
Then the temptation of going back start eating a Nigga, trying to find many ways to see those bigger figures
Steady working a job at Burger King seeing five-fifteen, wondering how am I going to provide for my family and buy my girl that ring
But I try to avoid the stress and give my job my best, while asking the Lord is what I'm going through is just another test
Will it get greater later or do I have to go back, but thoughts of the joint make me say "I'm not going back!"

** [I'm not going back, I got to keep pushing forward, and I'm not going back, through the grace of the Lord ...]

This government system got a Nigga flying right, and if they pull techs and try to come and get me we are going to put up a fight
I been gone away from my kids like to long, and thoughts of wifey on the phone telling me she's going to be strong
But I know that she gets tired of stressing and being alone, which gives me another reason to do right and avoid the wrong
It's just that not being able to provide for my kids makes me feel lesser than a man, when society got me struggling doing whatever I can
Then that temptation starts to hunt me once again, as I sit back and sip my Seven-up and my Gin
Telling myself that I can go grab the nine and go hit this lick, it aint no body going to know, it will be real quick
But than I start to think about my loving kids, and more thoughts about that time when I did that bid
That's when I start to tell myself "Just relax," because not being able to be with my kids make me say ... "I'm not going back!"

*** [I'm not going back, I got to keep pushing forward, and I'm not going back, through the grace of the Lord ...]

Now, dear God, I want to tell you that I trust in you, and I'm asking you to please help me avoid these temptations because your word is true
And in 1st Corinthians your word teaches me that you'll give me a way around temptation, so Heavenly Father, what I'm trying to say is ...
"I'm trying to have patients!"
Because from my past experiences you were there for me, and I know you'll help keep me on the right track to be there for my family

And dear God I want to thank you for the good time and the bad, because if it wasn't for those I wouldn't be where I'm at
Even though Satan is bugging me to fall off the right track, but heavenly father through your grace, I'm not going back!

** *[I'm not going back, I got to keep pushing forward, and I'm not going back, through the grace of the Lord ...]*

SECTION FOUR
MY EPIPHANY OF DIRECTION /
REACH OUT

Ma' Life

I was once apart of
The problem,
Now I choose to become
Part of the solution.

DO YOU KNOW ME

You're not my brother, we don't share blood in existence, so don't talk to me like you know me then ask me for permission!
With strict precision …
Trying to tell me that my life is a mission …
And trying to judge me about my damn addictions …
"Leave me the hell alone!"
Run, skedaddle and get on about your business, your back yard is full of garbage but you claim that you're full of wisdom;
Walking around like you're high on your throne and this world is your kingdom, then when you see another you feel that you have to preach to them …
"Your priorities are messed up!"
Work on yourself before you try to lift another up, and maybe I'll check my surroundings and give a crying fuss, that that brother is a pimp and that sister is a slut …
And that sister is dying from aids because she loves to bone and suck …
All for the street life's glitz and glimmers …
Should I care that she likes to smoke weed and get drunk until she's hammered?
Then when she's in her drunken slump her male associates penetrate her shattered soul …
Raw flesh upon flesh in her temple's hole … "I don't think so!"
Their live are their lives and mine is mine, so don't ask me why I walked those streets so blind;
I mind my own business and you should do the same, you don't know me and I don't know you so stop pushing the blame …
Hold on … I just remembered something that you told me which is right, I, like many others have a mission in life;
We are the same and we do share blood, our ancestors shared the grief to leak tears, sweat and blood;
Being dragged through the mud's to the cotton fields, for ten cents a day getting paid as a slave …
Maybe this is why I turned a blind eye and talked to you in rage, and the pain of seeing reality unfold has my mind stuck in a cage …
So maybe you do know me …
Just as I write these prolific words you read them as if they were me, and as you stare me in my eyes I notice that I am in you and you are in me …
Your reflection in the mirror tells me that you are me!

CHAMELEON

Why do we hide our emotions behind masks?
Camouflaging our true intentions with suppose it be solid structures
Believing that we're supposed to be men of a strong accent
But not knowing that we're fooling ourselves to a certain extent

Why do we lie for no reason?
Spitting venom into the minds of those we love
Giving them a false hope of a better tomorrow
When tomorrow will just be a repeat of today
Who knows the true intentions of a mans third eye
When it causes peeks of mass destruction
Delivering painful blows to the gut of our feminine culture

The many colors we betray through different hours of the day
Makes me wonder …
"Are we who you say we are?"
So when does change come into affect
And will we ever give respect
To the women we unconsciously neglect?
"So what's next?"

How about I …
Come from behind my mask
And show you an example that will last
By altering my retched past

Exposing a chameleon for what he really is …
A lizard that slithers
And changes its many colors
Unlike so many others
This lizard just happens to be …
A brother of the Negroid color.

MONKEY SEE THEN MONKEY HAD TO DO

To embrace the streets is to accept the consequences,
Once you reach prison you develop a conscious;
See ... the streets was my role model and the trays was my family,
The drugs, guns and gangs numbed me of reality;
I rolled with some of the toughest and followed most of the badness,
And most of the things that I did back then I now see it were madness;
I've burned so many bridges and sold to my own blood,
I was a beast that needed to be tamed as I marched through that sinking mud ...
Into the pits of destruction, I was young and lost,
Now I am found and loyal to the cause;
I know where I went wrong; I followed the wrong crowd,
Now I lead a life of redemption that would make my mother proud;
Sitting behind rusted bars, I know what I went through ...
It was all a case of monkey see, then monkey had to do!

I CRAPPED OUT

Damn, why these dreams playing tricks with my mind, my son growing up leading a life quite similar to mine;
I got out of prison and talked to him face to face, and he spoke to me like a stranger from some far distant place;

"Where were you when I needed you, and you were never around!"

His words were like daggers striking my heart on the ground;
I couldn't muster the energy to tell him of my past at that time, that I lived a life of rebellion, a life of brutal crime;
He was looking as if he was starring straight through me, and then turned away like he didn't know me;

He walked into the basement as I flopped down on the couch, and sat in deep thought for a moment but couldn't breathe and had to step out;
Looking across the alley to the park on the next block, seeing victims and villains of my past as I reached to my hip for my Glock ...
But the thought of my kids made me stop;
I did a one-eighty spin and walked back into the house, then followed my son's foot steps into the bottom section of the house, where I discovered him shooting dice with neutral members of my past ... [I thought] "Damn, I should kick your young ass!"
Rage, pain and hurt, you deceived me, and love for a child who I don't want to grow to be like me ... but he's following in my tracks;
"What do I have to do to get him back on the right track?"
Then what I saw next really messed me up, my son smoking weed and blowing the dice for luck ...
So I ran down the stairs to break the dice game up, rushed toward the crowd and chased them all away, then turned towards my son and he blew smoke in my face and said ...
"Lucky f***ing seven ... Lucky f***ing seven ..."
Aint that some stuff?

MENTAL WORKSHOP

How can I coupe with living amongst you when my mind isn't normal and my thoughts are un-pure?
I'm not in a sane state when it comes to the actions that I take, to make rational decisions when opportunity and I come face to face …

Most of the time I just want to be alone, so leave me be, because if I lash out I'll be on my way back to the penitentiary …

I can't continue to fool myself … there is something wrong with me mentally … I need help but I rather stay close to me, where no one can judge, laugh at or harm me …

This can't be human to think like me, I have to be mentally challenged -or in simple terms- crazy …
I put my faith in others but it seems as if they betray me, so … the only thing that's left is to stick to me … live within my own mind and step away from their reality …

Stepping inward for a while freely away from bondage … so maybe I do need physical captivity … because if I continue to live in your world, I might hurt someone in my acts of lunacy!

YOUNG BLACK SISTER

Why are you degrading yourself in such a manner, you got everyone on the streets calling you a Runner?

You're disturbing your temple and constantly putting yourself at risk, but the thing that you fear most is a H.I.V. test;

You're out there hustling, smoking weed and even popping Ecstasy, while downing yourself by saying "I'm that gangsta' bitch!"

When you turn your back, you're being laughed at and the guys are debating who gets the next stick;

If you don't believe me, I use to be one of those guys, out there selling drugs while wondering who was going to be the next hood-rat I get high … all for a little penetration;

The worst part about this is that there are guys in their thirties, looking for a young teen like you who gets down and dirty;

No condom, there busting all up in your temple, while giving you diseases that will leave you blind or crippled;

And when you tell one that you're pregnant he laughs in your face, and then tells you it's not his and race away;

It's time to change your ways of thinking baby-girl, if you plan to survive in this cruel world …

See drugs push your addictions to progress, evolving into others, more or less;

Then slowly you'll find yourself drifting away, lost in the abyss of a prostitutions maze;

Names like Runner, Hood-Rat, Bust-Down, Chicken-Head and Scoochy-Rat … are some of the names they title you with;

Because you're constantly out there having unprotected sex, and not know who your partner last had sex with … or better yet, they're constantly out there having sex with you and not knowing about all the partners that you've been with too, or the things that you would do;

Just think for a second and tell me that this isn't true, what would you do if a well dressed guy with lots of money in a nice car approached you?

Just as I thought, you would oblige with his advances, just for his finances, and not worry about the chances of you catching a disease …

Next thing you'll tell yourself is that "He dropped something off in me!"

Now you're walking around with an incurable disease, all because you were in heat for a little money …

Now that's messed up … you're so misguided and need someone to truly trust, and talk to you without acting upon lust …

So I am here for you … talk to me and tell me what's really wrong with you, and I'll speak my mind while giving you the un-cut truth, then look you in your eyes and ask you "What are you going to do … about change?"

Don't think because I want to help you it's strange!

We need to lift up all of our young sisters and help you all along the path that was paved for you since the beginning of time, so let's show the world that you can shine, by proving to yourself that you haven't run out of time …

[I see your tears!]

Don't think it's strange that you feel the change;
It's time to stand strong and take your place at your throne …
My African Queens!

SECTION FIVE
A TRUE EYE OPENER/
I SEE CLEARLY NOW

Our youth is hungry
And in dire need …

To be guided in a direction
Where they can succeed …

A future with goals
Is what they will learn
And respect from many
Is what they will earn…

Giving them the keys
To our historical what was …
Is to show them our pure uncut love!

SAY NO

Looks like that girl got Alex, just gain balance like Malcolm X and flex that mental muscle through that solemn text;
Then gaily stand tall with your head held high, and step back while telling yourself to put down those white lines …

It's a crime to self, it's bad for your health, just look at our history of self, and those who continued ended up getting nailed …
To a hell or a grave and developed those shakes until their minds were baked or their souls escaped …
Corporeal capacity, a life of immortality;
This may seem fake but it's reality, roaming across the galaxy …
Seeking ways to get back, but their flesh is what's lacked, and there is no coming back;
So the extremes I go, just to let you know, that this isn't the way to go, and a little knowledge to know is to just say "No!"

See, James Brown said "Get down!" and Frankie Lymon got down;
The god father of soul let it dig him a hole, but he regained control and found a direction to go, rest in peace to his soul, his legacy is a force …

Frankie rode the white horse, through his veins that venom poured in to eat his insides, the oldies was his life, but that's what he sacrificed, when he let that poison enter him it took over his life;
But now his name still lives on, even though he is gone, "Rest in peace Frankie Lymon" the world said then moved on …

These examples of such can never be too much; I just gave you a touch to see their lives were rough …
From those poisonous white lines that corroded the right mind, and lost direction to go, many hung their selves with those ropes, and realized it was Coke, or maybe it was Dope, that girl and boy is not a joke …
So get rid of the urges to pick up and just say "NO!"

NIAGARA

Hearing tha' sound of you, beating upon tha' rocks as you, flowed gently down stream ... only if you knew that you were in ma' dreams
To smell tha' aroma of, the fresh riva' wata' ma' love, resides on tha' otha' side ... Ms. Harriet Tubman has told me that this is most likely where maz' freedom resides ...

We would run and we would hide, in tha' church all times of nights, until tha' coast was clear ... and when we tried to escape we were full of fear
But in our minds that ambition to proceed on wit' our mission was evidently clear ... and you know wha' happen next cause you wha' diar'

Seein' clearly within our souls to feel those emotions that we couldn't control, as a light mist sprinkled upon tha' abyss of our souls
Tha' ripples in yo' wata' knew the way we would go ...

Across tha' bridge to a, beautiful place of love, and into tha' arms of a ... kingdom of love ...

Now I know that you knew this was wair' our freedom was ...
This here soil in ma' grasp represents no mo' slavery ... Canada, Canada, sweet Canada ...

TRUE MEANING IN BLACK AND BROWN

Caramel dark and chocolate smooth, deeply driven all the way down to the root; the pride that's always written upon our faces, to be the strongest amongst many different races ... "Black is beautiful!"

To know where you come from is to know where you stand, to proclaim that we're free is to stick to the plan; so know your strength is as strong as you make it, when we stick together we will always make it, just because brown stands for strength ...

The undying desire to overcome segregation, integrating into the abyss of capitalism and to be known as a survivor; when suppose to be justice holds us down we stand strong and unite as one; we're known as the minority, trying to stand strong against the majority to overcome this down played racism, just because we are filled with integrity ...

The beautiful look of full voluptuous lips and features that has evolved over time, that rich kingly hair that flows from our scalps and the creative styles that comes from the mother land ... Like corn rows to braid, afro's to fades and that pure natural cut ... "The texture of our being is pure!"

That native dancing like Latin prancing and the sound of voices that speaks with rhythm, this prideful culture will never die down just because of the strength in their brown; from the top of their heads to the nape of their feet, their prideful mentalities and Aztec roots shows true beauty ...

Their native tongues and intellectual speech, speaks highly in power to anyone they reach, just because of the charisma within them ...

"Black and Brown must be strong together!"

WHY SETTLE

She wants a brother with certainty and a mighty voice like Paul Robeson's, "Down by the river!"
Like the ripples beat the banks of the shore …

He wants a sister with soul and class like Maya Angelou, Gwendolyn Brooks and a touch of Nikki Giovanni …

She prefers intellect like Professor Michael Eric Dyson with a frame like Mike Tyson and the bravery and endurance of Arthur Ashe …

He prefers the woman-hood of Harriet Tubman with the audacity of Rosa Parks and a figure that was sculptured by Metta Warrick Fuller …

She listened to Ella Fitzgerald's jazz as she stretched in Yoga class while the notes seemed to invite her soul to comfort …

While he sat and read a book by Langston Hughes Dizzy Galesby played some tunes, on that vinyl as the needle smoothed through the grooves …

She said her good-bye's while leaving class but caught his eye as he walked pass and at that moment her heart sank into her stomach …

When the music came to a halt he decided to take a walk through the quiet but busy streets of the Windy City …

With a brief smile he nodded his head, continued to walk but felt a bit sad and second guessed himself for not turning around before continuing his stroll …

They shared similar dreams like Dr. King but walked pass each other on the street as they both suffered from Billy Holiday's type blues … but never realized …

That this sister and that brother had settled for another when the one they once sought after was each other.

IS THIS THE BEST THAT YOU CAN DO
A TRUE STORY

I remember a wise man stepping to me as I set writing at my center stage. He watched me for a moment as I wrote part of the formula to my future. Once I showed him that I noticed he was standing there, I said "What's up Hall!"

Hall was a twenty-seven year old self proclaimed genus. He would quote those exact words to many and they would all laugh at him, not taking him serious. I -on the other hand- gave him my full attention and grasped on to his every word like he sang a beautiful song that was food to my soul. Many would say that I was crazy, do to where we were … "Prison!"

I knew better than to judge a book by its cover or to believe what others would say. I knew what common sense meant, and my common sense would tell me that this young guy had plenty of knowledge. I admired what he had, and I wanted as much as I could get; so he always had my undivided attention. Besides, some of the most brilliant minds lay dormant behind those walls. They just made some detoured decisions in life that brought them to a punishable predicament.

This particular day I felt the need to listen, so I placed my pen beside my pad and leaned back in my seat as he pulled a chair up to my table.

"What you writing today?" He asked as he pointed his finger at my pad.

I looked down at my writing, then back to Hall as I said, "Just some poetry … you want to hear?"

He nodded his head in agreement and sat back as I spit each bar with rhythmic poise. Once I finished, I did what I always did afterward, wait and listen for a response of approval.

Hall just sat there as his eyes feel to the floor and crossed his arms across his chest. Nodding his head back and forward, his eyes slowly feel upon mine and I knew what was coming next. Those words that I couldn't stand to hear him say, "Is this the best that you can do?"

His face held a blank expression which I could never describe or decipher. Even though I felt as if I put my heart and soul into that poem, I proceeded to tighten up that poem and the many others that came before and after that day. Coming up with the same results from him; "Is this the best that you can do?"

Finally, I asked him, "Why do you always ask me that question?"

"You never know what you're capable of until you have given it your all. The only way that you know that you have given it your all is when you feel that you have put your best foot forward!" He stated as he focused in on my curious facial expression. "You never told me that it was the best that you could do, so I watched you continue to create art after art in an outstanding fashion. Now, I ask you once more, is this best that you can do?"

I was enlightened by his response and took a deep breath as I took his statements in. Then I sat forward myself and said, "This is the best I got for now … my heart and soul is in each and everyone of the poems that I have presented to you, but I know that I can probably quote them a bit better!"

The first smile I observed stretch across his face appeared as he looked directly into my eyes, giving me his full attention. "Then you deserve my honest opinion …" he stated as he began to nod his head back and forward again. "You've got a lot of talent and skill … and you know this. I personally like it, but you said that you could present it better. That is the true gist of the question that I continue to ask you … "Is this the best that you can do?"

HE'S GOT TO BE REAL

This day I saw the stars which was so beautiful,
Never looking into the eyes of God so clear before so had to embrace him.
I felt his presence somewhat and I knew that if He was as real as they say, He had to be listening. Every thought that I had was a bit fuzzy, but he knew what I wanted. He had to know! Life just didn't seem to be right at that moment for me, but greatness in this realm takes a lot of patients and time, a lot of which I don't have, but the creator has a plan for me!

Ever time I open my eyes another day, he lets me live in this project of a life not knowing but seeking some type of direction; but I think that he's about to open A door that will explode with good things for me and mine. I'm so misguided right now and he knows this, but he's letting me find my own way right now. I'm tired of seeking for direction and hitting brick walls; tired of trying to lead my own paths and ending on a foul note.

So when I looked into the sky seeing perfection in the stars, he lightened an eye of comfort for me. Giving me a better sense of awareness; only to know that tomorrow will bring me more outstanding moments. He's showing me that better days are ahead … only if I create them in him.

Helping the youth seems much like the life I need to embrace. I got to show them that I just came from under a world of lunacy from making my own stupid decisions in life. So for me to embrace Him is to know that a better road waits for me. After all, he did bring me through the fire and into a more sanctified position now. A place of solitude, so to say; a place that if I want to truly be a better man, all I have to do is look up and he will be there; embracing me with his warm and caring love. God is real … He just has to be!

ENLIGHTENMENT
A BIT OF HISTORY TO THE YOUNG BLACK MALE

Elder: "We are strong black men and must lift each other up. The knowledge of our African roots needs to be spread across our whole race!"

Young guy: "Why you say I'm from Africa and I never even seen the place?"

Elder: "Just look into the faces of your sisters and brothers and notice that you all closely relate!"

Young guy: "That's because we have the same mother and father, so what you getting at?"

Elder: "I am your brother and she is your sister, but we don't have the same birth mother and father, remember that!"

Young guy: "What do you mean we don't have the same birth mother and father and you ma' brother ... how you figure that?"

Elder: "Your true mother is a place where your ancestors were born and her name is Mother Africa."

Young guy: "I never lived there, nor ma' momma, grand-momma or even her momma!"

Elder: "But way before them you had a relative that was forced to aboard a ship, then chained and shackled to a post in the sub-level of that boat; with rows and rows of others chained from ankle to ankle and hip to hip ... tugging an oar and being beat with whips. The smell of rotten flesh and excrement in the air, and some of our cultural foods we have now came from way back there. The intestines of pigs were the waste that they were fed, and who can ever guess how greens became one; I would say that those who tried to escape came up with that one, with nothing to eat but the growth from the soil under nature's sun."

Young guy: "But what do that got to do with me?"

Elder: "Have you not heard anything? Your genealogy explains everything! So to further this truth many died on that journey, some were raped and killed and others died from burning. Those who stood up for their selves were tossed over board. Many thousands died from drowning by a supposed to be ship overlord. Those who survived this journey did it through faith, singing in unisons to communicate, 'stay strong my brothers and stay strong my sisters' was the true meaning and power behind the words they sang in unisons!"

Young guy: "So what happened next, I would like to learn?"

Elder: Once they reached land they were divided and sent too many different farms, to raise cattle, crops and pick cotton in the fields; plowing land that existed on the slave masters hills. At the end of there nights they were chained and caged in holes in the grounds, hearing their daughters and sons being raped in the slave owner's house. Not to mention the wives of the slave owners who demanded for sex; once the secret was revealed 'rape' was the only word that was said. The men were scorned, then beaten or hung to death; some had mutilation to their genitals for the lies of vaginal theft. That was a repeated cycle for many of years, their gain was our lost of blood shed and tears. Fast forwarding through time where our suppose to be 'freedom' came about. Where blacks were now able to rent our own apartment or house, in the slums of the cities and the gutters of towns, where there were only blacks and not a white person found; organizations were being built against the black men and the one that's popularly known is the Klue-Klux-Klan. Savages in white sheets disguising their faces, discriminating against every one of all other cultures and races ... burn crosses in the fields, yards and school in the black parts of town, even having the audacity to burn some African American churches down!"

Young guy: "Were there any people inside?"

"Many times there were, but most of the time they burned them at night, so their cowardness wouldn't surface when we put up a fight. All of these events took a toll and gave us strength, to fight for rights and make freedom permanent. We formed groups with cultural heads, men who spoke with power and helped each other through our stormy hours."

Young guy: "Men like who?"

Elder: Martin Luther King and Malcolm X, just to name two. They helped fight for our equality with religions on there back, Islam and Christianity to be exact. Malcolm X was a fighter who fought for our rights, through Islam he marched, rainy days and cold nights. While fighting violence against violence his vision of freedom went way beyond the shackles and chains. To stand strong against the oppressor for better living and jobs, where we could use our brain!"

Young guy: "And what about Dr. King?"

Elder: "See, equality was also the key for Dr. King, non-violence, but we marched in unison with many songs to sing. Making our voices heard with strength in our words, speaking with power and demanding what we equally deserved … 'Freedom, peace and justice for all!' as these events were taking place we fought through the chains and dogs. That was an on going cycle for many of years until one day they held back while we wiped away the tears, but the scares remain from the suffering and pain. Once the seventies came about, I know Malcolm X and Dr. King were turning in there graves. The decade of the pimp, coke and heroin came about, and influential movies that glorified this began to come out. Guiding our youth in a direction of tainted goals; buying and selling our own women and putting the drugs in our arms and noses. Destroying the hard work of those who fought for us to stay free, then the worst time that came about was the decade of the eighties. That's when the hip hop movement starting picking up off the ground, and many people were moved through the rhythm and sounds. The goal of this culture was to enlighten the minds of the youth, by exposing what our cultural heads went through and was trying to do. Groups like 'Public Enemy', 'Fight the Power' was their truth, and rapping words of power to anyone they reached to. As this era progressed crack-cocaine came about, and many young black men were brain washed into believing that this was a means of getting out, the ghettos, slums and downgraded parts of our societies; the living was unbearable for the African American families. That was the time when the real change came about and many found positive ways as a means of getting out."

Young guy: "You just gave me the whole history of a black mans tale!"
Elder: "That's not all just listen, there's more to tell … While freedom seemed clearer there were the nineties to fear of. When the oppressors seemed to totally raise their feet off of our necks we began to die off, killing each other for an unjust cause. Black on black crime became an all time high, the screams and wails of a black goddesses cries. It was a mother who was stressed out wondering why, her son had left the house and from a bullet he died. When we walked outside every corner sold drugs, and all was being sold by the neighborhood thugs. That era carried on from then until now, the major

problems we have now exists in our very own house. The choices we make every night and day, determines our future of being free or a modern day slave. See, some of us today has made choices and fail, that's why there are so many of us who are behind bars in jail; prison is a factor for many young black males, and our women are struggling and determined to prevail. Our kids are growing up with no male role models and ending up on a path that we left them to follow; bad choices, drugs, guns and gangs making our historical role models dreams vain. Just look into the eyes of your grandmother and see the pure uncut pain."

Young guy: "So what are you saying?"

Elder: "That we are blinded by the facts of our same selfish acts that we direct towards the next generation. Before I go, remember that enlightenment brings salvation … just open your eyes and receive as much as you can!"

Young guy: "I understand … I have to be a strong black man!"

THE CEASE OF THE BEAST

I see clearly at times, but the boggle intuitions of going back to a life style that brought me to this point fights intriguingly in my mind. I'm on the edge of not knowing if I should put my all into doing what I know is right … fighting this mental struggle, while taunting my self to fight.

So I ask myself "What kind of life could an ex-convict with a G. E. D. have in this economic struggle?" Not much from what I've seen. So do I go back to poisoning my own people to sow the riches of the field, while sacrificing my own freedom and the presence of loved ones? At the same time reaping the deaths and destruction of my own fellow African Americans … This is the war that is physical as well as mentally fought in the mind of myself.

Death, destruction, pain and humiliation in the eyes of those who really care for me, only if I go back to destroying my own communities … just for the riches of a bloodful dollar, and picturing myself riding slick while popping my collar.

Racing for materialistic and meaningless things in a world where it's now gangsta for a bird to sing. Cross roads of a mind that's blinded by time; constantly seeking to upgrade and not decline … to a life of struggle that feels like endless time … But it has to be the end of my old self, the cease of the beast.

MAKE UP YOUR MIND
TO ALL MY BROTHERS BEHIND BARS

There comes a time when one must ask themselves, "How much do I miss my family?"

Do you go back to society and do the same B.S. that brought you to the point of asking that question?

Just how much does it means to you?

Do you miss the presence of soft skin rubbing against your body, and that long silky hair that you massage your fingers through in a time of comfort?

How do you think she feels?

Pain, hurt and longing to reunite and obtain that passion that was once bestowed upon and within her … that intiment connection;

And your seed of reflection is misguided by some other man that takes your place in that domain that was once yours.

Missing those first steps, words and pitch with a baseball.

One must ask their self, "Do I regret that life style and everything that came with it?"

Only you can truthfully answer!

So what will you do?

You need to make up your mind fast because time is devouring your choices as rapid as the ending days!

SECTION FIVE
FINAL CALL / KEEPING STRONG

To succeed in this life
Black men must fight
Years of many wars.

AN EX-CONVICT'S DREAM

Physically incarcerated while working on a plan,
A plan to better himself any way that he can;
Exposing doors that exists in his mind,
Opening his eyes to a world that is blind;
Learning and teaching himself different trades,
Bettering himself for a path that is paved;
Paved with intentions to capture his dreams,
A road that is interceptive of an ex-convict's dreams;
So he creates more options to make it this time,
To lead a life more positive and no more crime;
Knowing that the strongest mental function that any being can have,
Is the will-power and imagination to create those paths;
When one door closes other options are available,
Because he built rooms of solid grounds and broke through walls to make his
life capable;
He's knowing that giving up is never an option in life,
So he flicked on a switch in his mind that was an overdrive light;
Not responding to derogatory and downgrading statements,
Because he knows that this time he's surely going to make it;
"Maybe I can be an Author and a Poet too!"
So he makes his great plan about what he will do;
That voice in his head gives him direction for tomorrow,
He speaks of his plans highly while others sulk in pity and sorrow;
Observing many people around him not trying to change,
Saying "I will be different and break that rigged cycle of chains!"
Staying positive and open minded is always the key,
So he works on himself positively while patiently waiting for his plans to peek.

"Hard work, patients and dedication is always the key for
Everyone's hopes and dreams to prosper!"

DIRECTION

How much loneliness can one man take when his heart is shattered and bruised?

He's on a verge of picking himself up but really don't know what to do

'Change' is really on his mind but negativity pulls him back

Then discouragement takes its toll again and opportunity is once again lacked

A new lead, new life, new direction and sacrifice is what he must now understand

Being real to himself before anyone else is what makes him a far greater man

The choice's he makes determines his fate and helps him to accomplish a goal

Then knowledge is gained and far less pain as he takes a path that gives him control

Everything that he seeks will find itself creep into his immortal soul

Then his mind will slowly begin to unravel and climb out of its mental hole

The power that he's yearned has now seemed to have burned its way into his life

Because he knows that the road he choose gives him direction to continue the fight!

> "Life is full of choices ... The choices are paths that lead to roads ...
> The roads are directions towards freedom or captivity- either   mental,
> spiritual, or physical!"

THE VOICE OF COMFORT

The joy of having a mother in your corner when one phone call puts you back on track

The rightful place of your goals and dreams that you unconsciously seem to have lacked

That voice lets you know that love is in your corner and will always be there until the bitter end

She tried her best to raise you up on a track of a strong black man

Rebellious to positivity because you wanted to make your own mistakes

When you finally opened your eyes to reality you thought that it was then too late

Even though you fell hard to the pavement she was there to help you up

And she gave you only as much as she could while giving you her motherly trust

She's just a mother to many but a goddess to you in every since of the word

Even though she expected more from you, you will always have her love …

So when you feel down and times are hard just know that you are never alone …

Just wipe your tears because your mother is near all you have to do is pick up the phone …

MY PRIDE AND JOY

The love that uplifted my soul
This inceptive inception which makes me bold
My everlasting pride and joy
A new life with my six month old boy

The first vision of my reflected image
Brought stronger faith deep within me

The hardest thing that I could ever bare
Was that two inch thick glass
And all I could do was stare

As I blinked the future went through my mind so fast
I blinked once more and it turned into the past

My son will grow strong and bold as an ox
With his father by his side when I leave this celled box

The time is coming soon and I can't wait
To hold him and feed him knowledge from my mental plate
With me in his life from that point on until the end
I will never leave his side because my heart feels as if it's a sin

I just pray he knows I love him and I want him to know
Sooner than later my presence will grow ...

MYYA

You are a beautiful ray of light when my darkest hours are about,
The beginning of a new me when I have dragged my life through the mud's
of wasteful endings ...
To tell you that you mean the world to me can only be an understatement,
Because my actions towards you will reveal all clues by letting you know that
we will make ...
A pure reflection that I give protection and dedicate my life to,
I forbid to divide and leave your side again and will never let any harm come
to you ...
I promise I will never let you go through what I went through ...
A fatherless child seeking direction from a man and woman that didn't know
affection,
And only knew how to get satisfaction from their own selfish drug addicted
actions;
Love was in their hearts but drugs strayed their focus,
And wanting a healthy life wasn't like a magicians 'hocus-pocus';
Then discipline would come from the strike of a cord,
A television, radio, or an iron on a board;
The bruises and welts from the cords and belts still remain on the surface of
my heart,
But deep down inside I have to let go so my past won't tear us apart;
You're the glimmer that shivers and the reason I've cried so many rivers as the
corner of my eye sockets leaked,
And you're my healer, soul sealer, a natural pain killer, so I'm glad that you are
the gift that my life has now reaped ...
Your presence creates my world because you're my baby girl and love is always
felt when togetherness is acquired,
You're a princess, my child, which drives my heart wild and baby girl you
make me so proud ... my Myya!

A NEW BEGINNING

The things we dream and the things we see, are the past, present and today's reality; slowly unfolding to the naked eye, and revealing souls piercing through the skies; benevolently gratifying ones subconscious cravings and lifting a being to a higher plain.

Resistance and persistence falls along those unconscious lines, and to give but deny was the immortal high; an imminent disaster that immerses the soul, as a weeping repentance opens eyes that are cold ... sweats which make the sheets wet and sticky; picking layers from the flesh, wiping drool that is fresh; gazing through the pitch black seeing but a glimpse of four walls ... what once felt so big now seems so small.

Being boxed in to this earth as the sun crumbles like dirt and relinquish all of its gases leaving ice on the crust; "I'm so cold and lonely, can someone save me ...?"

Dream within dream, evolving into new things; I'm a rose, now a bee, yet a wasp, now a tree; what's happening? My roots are forming through the ice and it's burning; as I struggle to get free the ground grabs a hold of me while my roots form through this whole plantation; My arms freeze, I can't move, and I don't know what to do, "Why cast me to this earth's damnation ...?"

I can't see to my sides, or my back, "Am I alive?" screaming Help me to be more as I cry ... Years seem to have past as I adapt to this darkness at last; the past sticks within me with no fears, then a deep voice appears saying "Let there be light!" and it's bright; focusing my vision and I notice my mission, in a field that has many more trees, but I ... I am pure beauty ...

My leaves are like silk, my bark is rough but smooth and my sap is the sweetest of its kind, now the ice melt from the sun's new glistering shine ...

Now the flowers rapidly bloom, there's daisies and lilies around every tree, but the purple's and red's of the roses are attracted to me; A flock of birds are coming and there goes some squirrels running, as two birds land gently on my being ... Its chirp's turns into words and what I think that I heard is "This is now a new beginning!"

LEGACY

When I die just give the tribe my ... last dying wish, and fill their hearts with the essence of my spiritual intent;

Let them know that I felt no pain and this was surely meant to be, for my last journey was not in vain it was a mission well complete;

I saw them all and gave the world everything that I could give, feeding life with sacrifice for my kids and I could live;

A harmony or melody that stayed in tune with many souls, humming birds and buzzing bees were like fuel when it flowed;

A poetic sense of imminence that guided me through this life, which triggered the Fourth-Dimension with persistence to further write;

Deep in thought to figure out what this life was all about, months had past and years flew by as I finally figured out ... The children's future is the task that deserves all the clout;

Carry on what I leave behind, it's well wroth the time; and continue to follow through by developing those fruitful minds;

So don't be sad this journey has ended because another one awaits, just know that it was all apart of heavens graceful fate ...

"Until we meet again!"

BLACK INSPIRATION
A BIT OF ENLIGHTENMENT

Maya Angelou - (1928 -) Poet, autobiographer, playwright, actress; Just Give Me a Cool Drink of Water 'fore I Diiie (1971); (1971) Georgia, First movie screenplay by African American woman to be produced; Oh Pray My Wings Are Gonna Fit Me Well (1975); I Shall Not Be Moved (1990); Wouldn't Take Nothing For My Journey Now (essays, 1993)

Arthur Ashes - (1943 - 1993) Won U.S. Open tennis Championship (1968); Won Australian Open tennis Championship (1970); Won Wimbledon and World Tennis Championship (1975); Inducted into the Tennis Hall of Fame (1985)

Ella Fitzgerald - (1918 - 1996) Grammy Award winner (1959) Jazz Singer

John Birks "Dizzy" Gillespie - (1917 - 1993) Jazz trumpeter; leader of revolutionary Be-Bop style of jazz

Yolanda Cornelia "Nikki" Giovanni - (1943 -) Poet; Re: creation (1970); Black Feeling, Black Talk (1968); Blues For All The Changes (1999); Grammy nominated American poet, activist and author, Professor of English at Virginia Tech University in Blacksburgh, VA; Nominated for Grammy Award for best spoken word album (2004)

Billie "Lady Day" Holiday - (1915 - 1959) Rhythm and Blues; recorded "Strange Fruit," song with a political message about lynching (1939)
Langston Hughes - (1902 - 1967) Poet, playwright, novelist, short story writer, major influence in Harlem Renaissance; The Weary Blues (1926); The Dream Keeper (1932); Freedom's Plow (1943); Mulatto (play, 1935); Mulatto, first long running Broadway hit by an African American author; First African American author to make a living off of earnings from writing
Gwendolyn Brooks - (1917 -) Poet; 1950 Pulitzer Prize for Annie Allen; A Street in Bronzeville (1945); Aloneness (1971); Primer for Blacks (1980): Bronzeville Boys and Girls (1956)
Dr. Martin Luther King Jr. - (1924 - 1968) Central Civil Rights leader of the 1960's; Key figure in the Montgomery, Alabama bus boycott and other civil rights activities; recipient of the Nobel Peace Prize 1964); He

was formerly named Michael Luther King at birth -Jan. 15, 1924- but later renamed Martin; Assassinated in 1968

Rosa L. Parks- (1913-) Refused to give up her seat to a white man on the bus and spurred a successful movement, the Montgomery, Alabama Bus Boycott -Dec. 1, 1955; (1996) Civil Rights Activist

Paul Robeson - (1898 - 1976) Concert singer [bass-baritone], actor; Body & Soul (1926), Show Boat (1936), King Solomon's Mine (1937), Native Land (1942); Played Othella on American stage with white cast (1943); Theater (1945)

Mike Tyson (1966 -) Heavyweight Champion (1985); Consolidated Heavyweight Crown (1987-90, 1996); Nick-named "Iron" Mike Tyson for his solid build and first round knock outs; Boxer

Harriet Tubman - (1820 - 1913) Once a slave who had escaped from a Maryland plantation in 1849; A bounty had been put on her head but she returned to the South as many as nineteen times to lead slaves on the Underground Railroad; She alone escorted roughly 600 slaves to freedom, which makes her one of the best known conductors' of the Underground Railroad.

Meta Warrick Fuller - (1877 -1968) Recognized as a sculptor at the Pennsylvania School of Industrial Art; she created a sculptor that was eight inches high titled "Man Eating His Heart" or "Street Sorrow" which caught the eye of then France's grand master, Auguste Rodin. With Rodin's blessing, Meta Warrick soon established a studio in the French capital and was invited to exhibit in the great solons.

Malcolm X - (1925 - 1965) Before converting to Islam, Malcolm's last name was 'Little', which was the name of the slave master who had long ago given his name to Malcolm's ancestors; In later years, during a visit to Mecca, Malcolm took on the name El-Hajj Malik El-Shabazz, which was given by the Muslims to those who had made the pilgrimage to Mecca; -Nation of Islam minister; Social Activist; Assassinated in 1965.

I thank them all for giving me a better sense of direction and helping me to focus on a better tomorrow. They all have a history of creating standards by moving through the road blocks that were set in front of them and I admire that. I, like them have had major road blocks in my path, but with there inspiration I chose to overcome.

Like William Shakespeare said, *"The world is my stage and all the men and women are merely critics ... "*